# How to read a
# Coat of Arms

# HOW TO READ
# A COAT OF
# ARMS

Peter G. Summers, FSA, FHS

illustrations by
Anthony Griffiths, BArch

Harmony Books/New York

Published in the United States in 1987 by Harmony Books,
a division of Crown Publishers, Inc., 225 Park Avenue South,
New York, New York 10003 and represented in Canada by the
Canadian MANDA Group


This edition originally published in Great Britain by
Alphabet & Image Ltd., Alpha House, South Street, Sherborne
Dorset, DT9 3LU

HARMONY and colophon are trademarks of Crown Publishers, Inc.

Manufactured in the United Kingdom
Library of Congress Cataloging-in-Publication Data
Summers, Peter G.

How to read a coat of arms.

1.  Heraldry.    I.   Title

CR28.S86 1987        929.6        87-228
ISBN 0-517-56667-2
10  9  8  7  6  5  4  3  2  1
First American Edition

# Introduction

There are many excellent handbooks on heraldry. This small book is not intended in any way to compete with these, but sets out to fulfil two purposes. First of all, it has been the writer's endeavour to provide the minimum amount of information to enable anyone ignorant of heraldry to take the first step towards 'reading' a coat of arms; and, secondly, to stimulate an interest in the subject, for a full understanding can only be acquired by further study. The reader will find here no lengthy list of heraldic charges or rules. Only the bare essentials are given, enough to ensure that any rough sketches made (and these can be perfectly adequate) include all vital details. This is necessary, since in heraldry details may be all-important for identification purposes, whilst some more dominant features may be of only minor significance. Much time can be saved when recording heraldry by knowing what should be included and what can safely be omitted. Variations arising from artistic licence are of no importance, but they may be confusing to the beginner; the ability to distinguish between these and true heraldic variants can only be acquired by experience.

# Chapter I. Reading a coat of arms

The term 'coat of arms' normally implies a shield, charged with heraldic devices. In its wider sense it also embraces the helm and crest, mantling, motto and other embellishments which make up a full heraldic 'achievement'; and these, though subordinate in interest and importance, must also claim our attention. Each will be considered in turn, starting with the shield.

## Shield

1. *Shape* The shape of a shield has no significance, though it can be of value for purposes of dating. However, the arms of a widow or a spinster are always borne on a diamond-shaped 'shield', the heraldic lozenge (Fig. 1).

FIG.1

2. *Heraldic charges* As a general rule the choice of one device or another has been an arbitrary matter, subject to the approval of the College of Arms. A personal Grant may include a device relating to the applicant's profession, whilst institutions and corporations have often chosen devices alluding to their origin and purpose. Allusions and references are sometimes subtle and hard to detect, and this applies especially to canting (i.e. punning) coats which have always been popular. The Bowes-Lyon family bears a lion for Lyon and bows for Bowes; but some other coats are less obvious, such as the pike (lucies) of the Lucy family, and the swallows (hirondelles) of the Arundells of Wardour.

Dexter  Sinister

FIG.2

3. *Impalements* A shield divided vertically with each half bearing a separate coat of arms almost always indicates a marriage, the dexter half bearing the husband's arms, the sinister half the arms of the wife. This is known as an impalement (Fig. 2); the husband impales his wife's arms. Rare exceptions to this rule are the arms of bishops, whose personal arms

may be impaled by those of their Sees. The same principle applies to the heads of Oxford and Cambridge colleges, officers of the College of Arms, and to holders of some other official positions. The arms of more than one wife can be shown, but as instances of this nature occur most frequently on hatchment the various methods of indicating them will be given in that chapter.

*Dexter* and *sinister* indicate right and left, but from the point of view of the person holding the shield and standing behind it. Therefore, when facing the shield, the left half is the dexter, the right half the sinister.

**4.** *Quarterings* A shield divided into four or more divisions, each bearing a coat of arms, is known as quartered, and the divisions are known as quarterings (Fig. 3). Invariably the first coat of arms and sometimes the last is the paternal coat; the others are coats inherited by marriages with armigerous heiresses. Some families are entitled to a large number of quarterings. In this connection 'heiress' has no financial significance, the inheritance of arms being from a family who have no male heirs to carry on the family name and coat.

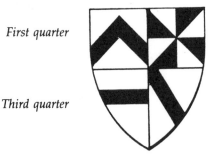

First quarter    Second quarter

Third quarter    Fourth quarter

8    FIG.3

FIG.4

5. *Escutcheon of pretence* This is a small shield placed in the centre of the main shield, and usually indicates a marriage to an heiress (Fig. 4). This bears the arms of the wife, which her descendants are entitled to bear as a quartering.

6. *Cadency marks* are very small heraldic charges usually placed in the centre of the upper part of the shield. They are used to denote the seniority of each member of a family, and also, but less frequently, to distinguish one branch of a family from another. In English heraldry nine different charges are used (Fig. 5). These cadency marks are not used in Scottish heraldry, where an alternative system applies. In both English and Scottish heraldry the head of the family bears an undifferenced shield.

FIG.5

Eldest son    second    third    fourth    fifth

sixth    seventh    eighth    ninth

9

7. *Marks of illegitimacy* Any consistency in marks of illegitimacy is of comparatively recent origin. A frequent misnomer is the term 'bar sinister' as a mark of bastardy, for it does not exist, the bar in heraldry being horizontal and thus neither dexter nor sinister. A bendlet sinister (Fig. 6) or a baton sinister (Fig. 7) appear as a mark of bastardy upon the arms of natural sons of a number of British monarchs or of their sons. This mark is then borne by their descendants. The arms illustrated in Fig. 7 show the baton sinister upon the arms of the Duke of St Albans, a descendant of an illegitimate son of Charles II by his mistress Nell Gwynne. The customary marks used in other instances of illegitimacy are, in England, Wales and Ireland, the bordure wavy (Fig. 8), and in Scotland the bordure compony (Fig. 9). It must, however, be stressed that there is no firm rule; the presence upon a shield of a bordure wavy does not of itself imply illegitimacy, and caution is therefore necessary.

FIG.6

FIG.7

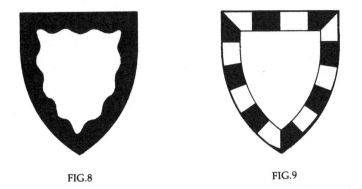

FIG.8 FIG.9

8. *Baronets* (other than baronets of Nova Scotia) bear on their arms the distinguishing mark of a small white shield charged with a red hand (Fig. 10). Sometimes, especially if the arms are quartered, it may be seen placed centrally. In such instances it must not be confused with the escutcheon of pretence (see 5). The badge of a baronet of Nova Scotia

FIG.10

FIG.11

consists of the arms of Nova Scotia, ensigned with a royal crown and suspended below the shield from a ribbon (Fig. 11).

9. *Augmentations* do not form part of the original coat of arms. An augmentation is granted in recognition of some special deed or service, and generally takes the form of an additional charge alluding to it. Nelson was granted two such augmentations to his family arms. The illustration (Fig. 12) is of the augmentation granted to the Lane family of Kings Bromley by Charles II, in recognition of Jane Lane in assisting the king to escape after the Battle of Worcester. It consists of a canton bearing the arms of England.

FIG.12

FIG.13      FIG.14      FIG.15

## Helm

This varies according to rank. A commoner's helm is in profile with the visor closed (Fig. 13). The helm of a knight or baronet is shown full-face with the visor open (Fig. 14); and a peer has an open barred helm in profile (Fig. 15). In English heraldry a helm in profile is almost invariably facing to the dexter. The difference in helm according to rank dates from Jacobean times. Before then there were no restrictions on their use.

## Crest

The device borne on the helm (Fig. 16), originally an additional means of distinguishing a warrior in battle or a competitor at the tournament. Below the crest is the wreath or torse (always with six twists), derived

FIG.16

13

FIG.17

from the piece of silk which hid the join of the crest to the helm. Alternatives to the wreath, though not so frequently seen, are the chapeau or cap of maintenance (Fig. 17), and crest coronets (Figs 18, 19, 20). The latter are not indicative of nobility, and should not be confused with peers' coronets, which will be referred to later. Some families (though not always with authority) use more than one crest. The hatchment of General Sir Love Parry Jones-Parry in the parish church of Llanbedrog, North Wales, shows five! *

FIG.18

FIG.19

FIG.20

*No heraldic device has had its meaning more abused than the crest. Any reference in the press, and elsewhere, to a crest will almost invariably be found to refer to a coat of arms.

14

FIG.21

FIG.22

# Mantling

The slashed and swirling drapes flowing from the helm and forming a decorative framing to the arms (Fig. 21) derive, as the wreath, from actual usage, in this case from the cloth which hung from the wreath and protected the back of the wearer's head from the heat of the sun. Occasionally it may be seen as a plain cloth without any decorative treatment (Fig. 22).

# Peer's mantle

The achievement of a peer is often found displayed on his mantle or robe of estate. This practice may be noted especially on coach panels and on hatchments.

15

# Supporters

These, as the name implies, are figures flanking the shield and supporting it, such as the lion and unicorn of the Royal Arms. Few commoners have a right to supporters, though peers have always been entitled to them. They are much in evidence nowadays in civic heraldry and the arms of corporate bodies.

*Baron*
FIG.23

*Viscount*
FIG.24

## Peer's coronet

A coronet of rank is normally placed above the shield (Figs 23-27).

*Earl*
FIG.25

*Marquess*
FIG.26

*Duke*
FIG.27

# Motto

In English heraldry a motto does not, as the arms and crest, form part of a Grant, and may be changed at will. However, this rarely happens and the same mottoes have been used by many families for generations. The use of more than one motto is not unusual.

# Orders, medals and other insignia

The shield of a Knight of the Garter is surrounded with the Garter (Fig. 28). Knights of all other Orders surround their shield with the ribbon or circlet of the Order, bearing the Order's motto. In such circumstances the arms cannot be impaled. If the holder of the Order is married, the usual practice is for the wife's arms to be impaled with his on a second shield surrounded with an ornamental wreath. Medals are shown suspended on ribbons below the shield; and the pastoral staves of bishops are placed in saltire (that is, in the form of a St Andrew's Cross) behind the shield.

FIG.28

17

# Chapter II. Funeral hatchments and armorial panels

This section has been included for two reasons. First, because church guides and books on church architecture and furnishings rarely give either armorial panels or hatchments more than a passing reference; and, secondly, because the majority of hatchments, being unassociated with any inscriptions, will be foremost among the coats of arms the church visitor may wish to identify.

The diamond-shaped hatchment derives from the medieval achievement: the crested helm, shield, sword, etc., carried at the funeral of a knight or noble, an excellent example of which may be seen over the tomb of the Black Prince in Canterbury Cathedral. The diamond hatchment, with which we are concerned, originated in the Low Countries and first appeared in England in the early seventeenth century, and though it was sometimes carried in the funeral procession the custom was for it to be hung on the front of the house during the period of mourning, and thereafter placed in the church. It consists normally of a full heraldic achievement painted on a wood panel or canvas. Early examples are small, from two to three feet square, in narrow frames often decorated with skulls, crossbones, hourglasses and other emblems of mortality. Late eighteenth-century and nineteenth-century hatchments are larger, in wide frames sometimes covered in black cloth, with cloth rosettes at the corners. Early hatchments are almost invariably well painted in a bold and vigorous style, in marked contrast with the poor quality of many of nineteenth-century date.

The background on a hatchment is an important and unique feature for it is always painted black behind the arms of the deceased only, the remainder of the background being left white. The hatchment of a bachelor or spinster will thus have an all-black background. The hatchment of a husband or wife will have the background black only on the dexter or sinister halves respectively, and the background on the hatchment of a widow or widower will be all black. Non-heraldic, purely decorative features appear on hatchments of all periods. Cherubs' heads are very common, especially when taking the place of the crest on the hatchment of a woman; skulls are often found in the bottom corner, below the motto. Flags regularly occur on the hatchments of high-ranking military and naval officers. A special reference should be made to mottoes on hatchments; for, although sometimes the family motto is used, more frequently an appropriate sentiment, such as *Resurgam, Mors Janua Vitae* or *In Coelo Quies* is seen. Occasionally both family and funeral mottoes are found together.

In Chapter I it was explained how a marriage is shown, but this referred to one wife only. If a man has married twice, the usual practice is to display the arms of both wives, and there are several methods of so doing, none of which is rare. In the first three instances (Figs 29-31) the arms all

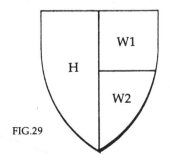

FIG.29

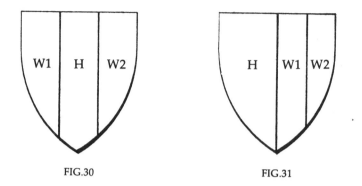

FIG.30                    FIG.31

appear on the shield. In the fourth, only the family arms appear on the main shield; but in the dexter and sinister angles of the hatchment are small panels, each bearing a shield, the dexter with the first wife's arms impaled, the sinister with the second wife's arms impaled (Figs 32, 33). In each instance the backgrounds are treated in the appropriate manner. The arms of more than two wives are rarely found on a hatchment; though at Moulton in Lincolnshire can be seen the hatchment of Henry Boulton, which shows the arms of all his five wives. He impales the arms

FIG.32         FIG.33

of his last wife on the main shield, and in each corner are placed the arms of each of his previous four wives.

There is not always a clearcut distinction between a hatchment and an armorial panel. The term 'armorial panel' here includes any heraldic board or canvas (other than the Royal Arms) not of diamond shape. However, there is some overlapping, for some seventeenth-century armorial panels without inscriptions, and with a black/white background, have almost certainly been used as hatchments; whilst some otherwise typical hatchments, which have at the base an inscription starting *Near here lies buried . . .*, come more readily into the category of armorial (in this case, memorial) panels. But the great majority of rectangular boards with coats of arms painted on them bear inscriptions which indicate clearly that they are an inexpensive form of memorial; others may commemorate church benefactors. Some of the early seventeenth-century uninscribed panels would appear to be a transitional form between the medieval achievement and the early diamond hatchment. No diamond hatchment has been recorded of an earlier date than 1627, whereas rectangular memorial boards date back to the sixteenth century.

The total number of hatchments and panels surviving in Britain is probably about five thousand. Armorial panels (mostly inscribed memorial boards) are especially common in Cheshire. Hatchments are widely distributed in England and Wales, though uncommon in Scotland and almost non-existent in Ireland. The peak year for those surviving is 1837; but a great many earlier ones must have perished, for canvas is particularly susceptible to damp, and many others were probably thrown out at the time of nineteenth-century church restorations. The period of greatest use was probably the late eighteenth century and the early nineteenth century. The custom is not yet completely obsolete, for there are at least a hundred twentieth-century examples, many of these being for heads of university colleges. One of the more recent hatchments is that of Sir Hereward Wake, in Courteenhall Church, Northamptonshire, who died in 1963. Hatchments may be found nowadays not only in churches, but also in country houses and many other secular buildings, including, in the writer's personal experience, a seaside hotel, a country pub, two girls' schools, a tea shop and a cave.*

Sometimes a series of hatchments is found commemorating several generations of the local lords of the manor; but this is by no means always the case. At Margate in Kent, for instance, there are twenty hatchments in the parish church, almost all belonging to different families, many of which certainly had only tenuous links with the town.

The Royal Arms, a mark of loyalty to the Crown, may be seen in many churches, dating from the reign of Henry VIII to that of our present Queen. They are generally rectangular and painted on canvas or wood panels. But examples do occur, and not uncommonly in the West Country, which look exactly like hatchments, even with a black background to the arms. However, many of them bear dates, which make it clear that their appearance belies them. Royal hatchments, though rare, do exist. Several, painted on both canvas and silk, are in the parish church at Kew, and a few others have been recorded from different parts of the country. William IV, who died in 1837, is commemorated by no less than four surviving examples. As 1837 is the peak year it would seem that his demise gave a temporary boost to the hatchment painting industry!

---

*The hatchment in the cave has, alas, perished. It commemorated a Dashwood baronet and hung until recently over a pool in one of the caves at West Wycombe, Buckinghamshire, a haunt of the Hell Fire Club.

# Chapter III. Recording a coat of arms

This should present no difficulty, so long as great care is taken. It is impossible to overstress the need for this care, and it is strongly advised that, once the details have been recorded, they should be checked to ensure that nothing has been omitted. A detail overlooked can cause much frustration later. There are two practicable methods of recording, both of which are perfectly satisfactory. By far the quicker is blazon (describing what is seen in heraldic terms), but this requires some experience and a basic knowledge of heraldry. The second method is by drawing the arms 'in trick'. This means a sketch with the colours indicated (Fig. 34), but provided that adequate descriptions are given the sketch · can be very roughly executed (Fig. 35). The vital point is that the person recording the arms should be able at a later date to know exactly what was on the shield.

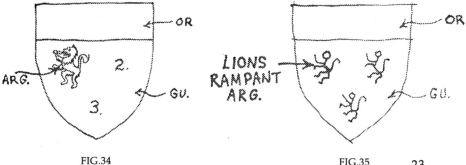

FIG.34                    FIG.35        23

The same principle applies to recording crests and supporters. The helm can be roughly sketched or described; it is important to know only whether it is full-face or in profile, and whether the visor is open or closed. The colour of the mantling should be noted, but no other details are necessary. The motto must, of course, be recorded, and details taken of any coronets, orders, medals and other insignia. The heraldic names for colours should always be used; the abbreviated forms are adequate if they are clearly written. Coats of arms are often found uncoloured. These may prove more difficult to identify unless they have the colours indicated by hatching, a system introduced in the seventeenth century. The technique is suited especially to engraving, and though most used on silverware and bookplates it may also be seen on eighteenth-century and later memorials. A key to the system (which is not recommended for use in recording), and a list of the heraldic names for colours, are given on page 37. Always use a notebook rather than odd pieces of paper which can easily be mislaid or lost. Binoculars and a torch can be a great help, especially in recording hatchments which are so often hung high up in dark places, such as the inside of the church tower. The date of viewing should be entered, as should the exact locality, the material used for the arms, and the technique employed (whether, for example, the arms are painted, carved or engraved).

FIG.36                                              FIG.37

# Chapter IV. Identifying a coat of arms

Success is the more likely to be achieved by a systematic approach, tackling the sources most readily available first. If the coat of arms is in a church, make sure there is no monument or tablet bearing similar arms. Even if one is discovered with the arms quartered or impaled, the inscription may solve the problem. Search the graveyard carefully; heraldic tombstones are by no means rare. Finally, after ensuring that no descriptive guide or leaflet for the church is available, make a list of all the principal names appearing in the churchyard, not forgetting names of benefactors and incumbents. The list will not be a very long one, as monuments bearing other coats can be ignored, as can the humbler gravestones.

The shape of the shield can be a help in dating. Most shapes were copied in Victorian times, but the first example shown (Fig. 36) would not have been used before 1740, and the spade shield (Fig. 37) was especially popular from about 1770 to 1810.* Sometimes the village pub will provide a clue; heraldic inn signs may survive long after the family they represent has left. Before leaving the village, it may prove worth your while to call on the incumbent. If he cannot help he will probably suggest that you call elsewhere, for there are few villages without a local antiquary.

This accomplished, your next visit must be to a reference library, one large enough to contain the county histories and the standard heraldic and genealogical reference books. Here the amateur herald will have the advantage over the layman; he will have recorded the arms in blazon and may not have found it necessary to take the steps so far described in this chapter. All he may need to do is to look up the arms in a work indispensable to him, Papworth's *Ordinary of Armorials*. Another indispensable work, Burke's *General Armory*, lists coats of arms under family names alphabetically. Papworth is Burke in reverse; the heraldic charges appear alphabetically, so that any coat of arms listed can be quickly identified. But to use Papworth's *Ordinary* some knowledge of heraldic terminology is essential. The layman can, however, tackle Burke's *General Armory* and look up all the names he has recorded; the coats of arms are heraldically blazoned, but there will be heraldry books readily available so that the meaning of the term can quickly be ascertained. County histories and, if available, parish histories should also be consulted; much heraldic and genealogical information will be found in them. The county or city record office may possess useful material in the way of parish registers (many incumbents have handed

*This variation in style is particularly noticeable in eighteenth-century armorial bookplates, which can themselves be a fruitful source of information, both heraldic and genealogical. The writer has more than once been successful in identifying a hatchment by a study of bookplates, when all other sources had failed.

over their early registers for safe keeping), armorial seals attached to old title deeds and marriage settlements, estate maps bearing coats of arms, and other helpful documents. There may be no need for so much research as this, but even if the arms have been successfully identified much more can still be done. The next step will be to try to identify the actual member of the family. Much will depend on whether a family of that name is found to have been resident in the district. If no pedigree can be traced (Marshall's *The Genealogist's Guide* and Whitmore's *A Genealogical Guide* list most known printed pedigrees, and the works in which they may be found, alphabetically under families), then the parish registers of the district should be studied.

Three further points remain to be made. First, many coats, especially on hatchments of Victorian date, were illegally assumed and never granted. It may, therefore, be virtually impossible to identify the families concerned in such instances as these. Secondly, the procedure for identification described above relates to a coat of arms seen in a church. Similar steps should be taken in the identification of a coat of arms on or in a secular building. The parish church, the county reference library and the local record office are the focal points of all local heraldry and genealogy.

On the following four pages are illustrations of four hatchments; much can be gained from them as a result of the information given in previous chapters. It is suggested that you try your skill in writing down all the details you can discover from them, and then check your findings with the descriptions on page 32. If you are successful then the first step in identification has been achieved. The second step will be discussed in the next chapter, *Further study*.

FIG.38

FIG.39

FIG.40

FIG.41

31

19723

# Notes on the hatchments illustrated on the four previous pages

FIG.38 The arms are on a lozenge and are impaled, and the background is all black, so the hatchment must be for a widow; the coronet indicates that her husband was a viscount. The hatchment is at Arley, Worcestershire, and is for Frances, daughter of Charles Sims, who married George, Viscount Valentia, and d. 21 January, 1856.

FIG.39 The arms are again impaled, but this time on a shield, and the sinister background is black, indicating the hatchment of a married woman. The dexter half of the shield bears the Badge of Ulster, so her husband was a baronet; the coronet shows that he was also a baron. The hatchment is at Huntingfield, Suffolk, and is for Maria, daughter of Andrew Thompson, who married Joshua, 1st Baron Huntingfield, and d. 7 December, 1811.

FIG.40 There is a quarterly coat on the main shield, and the background to it is all black, indicating that it is the hatchment of a man. The quarterings, only shown on the main shield, are inherited, and the Badge of Ulster indicates that he was a baronet. The two small shields to the dexter and sinister represent two marriages; the dexter to his first wife, the sinister to his second wife. The background to the sinister shield is black on the dexter side only, indicating that his second wife has survived him. The hatchment is at Brightwell, Suffolk, and is for Sir Samuel Barnardiston, 1st Bt., who married, 1st, Thomasin, daughter of Joseph Brand, and 2nd, Mary, daughter of Sir Abraham Reynardson, and d. 8 November, 1707, aged 88.

32

FIG.41 This is an unusual and most interesting hatchment. It shows two oval shields, each bearing impaled coats, the dexter surmounted by a mitre, and the sinister by a cherub's head. The dexter shield shows the arms of a bishop, impaled by the arms of his See; the background is white behind both coats. The sinister shield shows the arms of the bishop impaling the arms of his wife; the background is black behind her arms only, indicating that the hatchment is for her. The hatchment is at Babraham, Cambridgeshire, and is for Jane, daughter of General James Adeane, who married the Rt. Rev. George Henry Law, Bishop of Bath and Wells, and d. 27 September, 1826.

# Chapter V. Further study

The second step in reading a coat of arms cannot be covered by the scope of one small book, as much more knowledge will be required which can only be obtained from a heraldic textbook. In Chapter IV it was shown how some coats of arms, especially in churches, can be identified without any knowledge of heraldry, but there will be many coats which are not easy to identify and here a knowledge of heraldry will be essential. This applies particularly to coats of arms with no known provenance. How, for example, can one identify the arms on the panel of stained glass, the armorial plate or the cast iron fireback, bought at an auction or antique shop? In such instances, in order to identify the arms, one must be able to identify the various charges, and a substantial volume is needed to list them all. Apart from charges, which are purely heraldic, almost anything can be found on coats of arms; in fact, one would be hard put to it to find any living creature or inanimate object that has not appeared on the coat of some family or organisation.

The list of books on page 39 gives a wide variety to choose from. If you have by now become keen to learn more, then the purchase of one of the larger books is recommended, as it will be more comprehensive. Most of the larger libraries will have copies of Papworth's *Ordinary* and Burke's *General Armory*, as well as editions of Burke's *Peerage* and *Landed Gentry*.

# Chapter VI. Entitlement to arms

It may be that some of you have wondered, or are now wondering, if you are entitled to a coat of arms. To establish the right in England and Wales it is necessary to show that you are descended in the direct male line from someone who has been granted arms, or whose arms are officially recorded at the College of Arms. In Northern Ireland the same ruling applies, but the arms must have been officially recorded by Ulster King of Arms, whose original records are in Dublin. In Scotland, only the senior male representative (the heir male) bears the undifferenced arms, and for all other male descendants the arms can only be borne with difference marks, by application to the Lyon court — a process known as matriculation.

Such proofs of descent may, for some, not be difficult, but for others, who think they may belong to an armigerous family, it can be a long and expensive business; much research may need to be done and this may, of course, not be successful. However, the first step to take must be to consult members of your family; the more senior they are, the better. Most of us know the names of our grandparents, and where they came from; and, if you still have grandparents, great-uncles and great-aunts living, consult them first and you will then have traced your family back four generations. It may be they will themselves have been interested, and have some genealogical notes, or a family bible, which is so often used for this purpose. My advice is, do not put this initial research off; get all the facts you can from the family first, not forgetting dates and places of birth, and other relevant details. Facts which may seem unimportant at the time may prove vital later; it must be remembered that every stage in the descent must be provable by documentary evidence.

Finally, if all researches fail, all is not lost. Such experiences are commonplace, and applications to the College of Arms will always receive sympathetic attention. If consent is given to a Grant being made, fees will need to be paid, but as the Grant will confer a right to their usage to all the descendants in the male line, in perpetuity, the proportionate cost will indeed be small.

# Heraldic colours

Those most frequently used are:

METALS

gold = or

silver = argent (arg.)

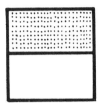

COLOURS OR TINCTURES

black = sable (sa.)

red = gules (gu.)

blue = azure (az.)

green = vert (vt.)

purple = purpure (purp.)

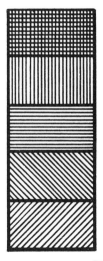

37

FURS

vair

ermine (erm.)

In addition to metals and tinctures, two 'furs' — vair and ermine (erm.) — are often met with.

The ermine is usually black on white, but it may be white on black, black on gold, or gold on black. Nowadays the varieties are normally blazoned 'sable ermined argent', etc.

NATURAL COLOURS

Any charge in natural colours is blazoned as 'proper' (ppr.).

# *Further reading*

*General*
There are many small and inexpensive handbooks which list heraldic terms and charges, and explain how to blazon a coat of arms; as, for example:
*An Outline of Heraldry* R. Innes-Smith, Pilgrim Press.
*Discovering Heraldry* Jacqueline Fearn, Shire Publications.
*The Observer's Book of Heraldry* Charles MacKinnon, Warne.
For those who wish to delve more deeply and acquire a more comprehensive knowledge, the following works should meet their needs:
*Boutell's Heraldry* revised by J.P. Brooke-Little, Warne.
*A Complete Guide to Heraldry* A.C. Fox-Davies, revised by J.P. Brooke-Little, Orbis.
*An Heraldic Alphabet* J.P. Brooke-Little, Macdonald.
*The Romance of Heraldry* C.W. Scott-Giles, Dent.

1987 sees the publication by Alphabooks, Sherborne, Dorset of *A New Dictionary of Heraldry*, edited by Stephen Friar, with numerous contributors.

*Identification*
Burke's *General Armory* and Papworth's *Ordinary of British Armorials* are expensive works and not entirely reliable, but are essential if much research is intended. The later editions of Fairbairn's *Book of Crests* contain an extensive series of plates arranged as an ordinary, and may be invaluable if a crest only needs identification, such as is frequently the

case with signet rings and silver. Most of the larger reference libraries will possess copies.

For those whose interest is aroused by hatchments, the series of volumes, *Hatchments in Britain*, ed. P.G. Summers (Phillimore), will be most useful and informative.

All the above books are available from the Heraldry Society, 44-45 Museum Street, London WC1, or from booksellers.

On the cover of this book, the arms above the author's name are those of the author. Above, on the left, are those of Sir John Tiptoft, K.G. On the right are the arms of Henry le Despencer, Bishop of Norwich 1370-1406, from his seal.